MAGIC FUN

By the editors of OWL and *Chickadee Magazines*

Edited by Marilyn Baillie

Little, Brown and Company
Boston Toronto London

First U.S. Edition 1992

The activities in this book have been tested and are safe when conducted as instructed. The publisher accepts no responsibility for any damages caused or sustained due to the use or misuse of ideas or materials featured herein.

First published in Canada in 1991 by Greey de Pencier Books

ISBN 0-316-67741-8 (hc)
ISBN 0-316-67739-6 (pb)
Library of Congress Catalog Card Number 91-75546
Library of Congress Cataloging-in-Publication information is available.

Joy Street Books are published by Little, Brown and Company (Inc.)

OWL and the OWL character are trademarks of the Young Naturalist Foundation.

Series design: Wycliffe Smith
Book design: Word and Image Design Studio
Photography: Ray Boudreau
Illustration: Josephine Cheng (pages 4, 5, 6, 7, 8, 9, 15, 18, 20, 22, 24, 25), Vesna Krstanovich (pages 10, 13, 16, 19, 23, 26, 30−31).

HC: 10 9 8 7 6 5 4 3 2 1
PB: 10 9 8 7 6 5 4 3 2 1

Printed in Hong Kong

Contents

Show Time

Hide and Seek . . . . **page 4**
Paper Pranks . . . . **page 6**
Mystery Box . . . . **page 8**
Mysterious Mixtures . . . . **page 10**

Body Magic

Baffling Body Tricks . . . . **page 12**
Tricky Fingers . . . . **page 14**
Eye Puzzlers . . . . **page 16**

Fortune Fun

Fantastic Fortune Cake . . . . . . **page 18**
Fast Fortune Flicker . . . . **page 20**

Card Capers

The 1, 2, 3 Card Trick . . . . **page 22**
Check the Deck . . . . **page 24**

Mind Magic

Mind Reading . . . . **page 26**
Magic Messages . . . . **page 28**

Trick Tips . . . . **page 30**

Hide and Seek

Now you see it, now you don't!

DISAPPEARING COIN TRICK

Make a coin disappear right before your friends' eyes.

You'll Need:

Old clear drinking glass
Newspaper
Construction paper
Pencil
Scissors
Glue
Coin
Scarf

The Setup:

1. Trace around the rim of the glass on a piece of construction paper and cut out the paper circle.

2. Squeeze some glue on newspaper and dip the rim of the glass into it.

3. Place the glue-rimmed glass rim-side down on the paper circle. Let it dry.

4. Before your friends arrive, put the trick glass circle-side down on construction paper of the same color as the circle.

5. Place a coin beside the glass, and cover the trick with a scarf.

6. Practice the trick until you can do it perfectly.

The Trick:

■ Tell your friends that you are going to make a coin disappear.

■ Lift the scarf to let the audience see the glass and coin.

■ Wave the scarf with one hand in front of the glass and chant:
"Abracadabra, abracadoo.
I am amazing and so are you."

■ At the same time, quickly slide the glass over the coin with your other hand. Whip the scarf away as you shout "Ta da!" The coin "disappears"!

■ Now make the coin reappear the same way.

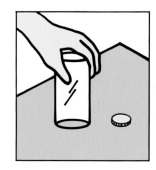

Show Time

Magic Challenge 1.

Can you move one of these coins so you make two rows of four coins each?

See page 32 for the answer.

Paper Pranks

With a snip, snip you can slip your body
through a postcard, or fit your head through
a small paper loop.

BODY SHRINKER

**No magic potions are
needed, just the magic
touch.**

You'll Need:

2 postcards, each 4 x 6 in.
Scissors

The Setup:

1. Fold one of the cards in half the
long way.

2. With the fold toward you, make
ten cuts. Leave 0.5 in. uncut at the
end of each cut.

3. Cut through all the folds, except
for the ones on each end.
4. With the folds away from you,
make more cuts between the ones
you have already made. Be careful
not to cut all the way through.

5. Open the paper carefully and
practice stepping through. Fold it up
again and put it aside.

The Trick:

■ Amaze your friends by announcing that you can fit your entire body
through a hole in a postcard.
■ Ask someone else to try it first.
Give them the scissors and an uncut
card.
■ When the trick seems too big a
task, pull out your card. Show the
audience that it is the same size as
the other. Then open up your card
and step on through.

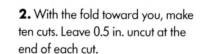
Show Time

LOOPY LOOP

Lengthen a paper loop to twice its size without adding any more paper.

You'll Need:

Newspaper
Scissors
Clear tape

The Setup:

1. Cut several strips of newspaper each 20 in. long and 3 in. wide.
2. Hold one end of a strip in each hand and bring the two ends together to form a loop. Give one end a half turn (the turn is very important) and then tape the ends together. (See picture.) Make another "magic" loop identical to this one.

The Trick:

■ Place the paper loop on your head and announce that you can magically make it fit over your head without adding paper, tape, or glue.

■ Cut the loop lengthwise down the center of the strip. Everyone will be amazed to see that the loop doubles its size. Now slip it over your head.

■ Your friends will be keen to try this easy trick. Hand one of them a newspaper strip that you quickly attach but do not turn. What happens when they cut? It's not so easy.

■ Mystify your friends with more paper magic. Take a second magic loop (that you taped earlier with a half turn). This time make your cut closer to the edge than last time. Keep cutting around and around until you end up exactly where you started. Now what do you have? One loop linked to another and the other is twice as big around as the original loop. It's a loopy loop!

Paper Makers
Who were the first paper makers?
Wasps!
A queen paper wasp makes her nest by shredding rotten wood and mixing it with her saliva. She does this over and over again to make enough paper to build her nest.

Mystery Box

Abracadabra! Reach right into your mystery box and magically pull things out of thin air.

You'll Need:

Cardboard shoe box with one of
   its short ends removed and saved
Scissors
Clear tape
Black paint and a paintbrush
Piece of cardboard the same length
   as the box but 2 in. wider
Second piece of cardboard big
   enough to make a front door
   for the box
2 rubber bands
4 paper fasteners
small items

The Setup:

1. Paint the inside of the box black and carefully cut two wide strips from the lid as shown. Tape the lid onto the box.
2. Paint both sides of the first piece of cardboard black. When dry, fold it in half the long way and slide it into the box as shown.

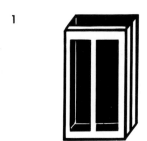

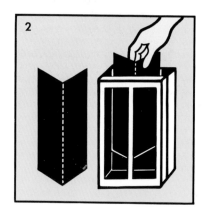

3. Make a front door out of the second piece of cardboard and tape it to the box. Tape the end back onto the box as a top flap.
4. Use the paper fasteners and rubber bands to make door and flap closers.
5. Before your friends arrive, stuff a few small things into the secret compartment at the rear. Close and fasten the door, then the top flap.

Show Time

The Light and Heavy Box

One famous magician astonished everyone with his magic box trick. The box was light enough for a small child to lift but it couldn't be budged by a big, muscular man. What was the secret? Under the platform the magician had placed an electromagnet! The box had a hidden metal plate. When an electric current was secretly switched on, the box stayed stuck to the platform.

The Trick:

■ Tell your friends that you can make objects magically appear from your mystery box.

■ Open the front door to show your audience that the box is empty. You can even stick your hand in to prove it.

■ Close the front door. Wave your hand over the box while you repeat a magic spell, then open the top flap.

■ "Ta da!" Pull out your hidden objects one by one.

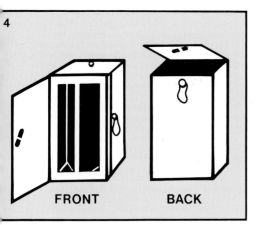

4

FRONT   BACK

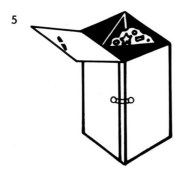

5

Mysterious Mixtures

Add mystery to your magic show with secret potions and spooky writing.

GHOST WRITING

Fool your friends with a foggy message from a friendly ghost.

You'll Need:

Magic mix (a drop of liquid detergent in a glass with a little water)
A nearby window or a mirror

The Setup:

1. Think of the name of a person who will be at your show. A short name works best.
2. Dip your finger into the Magic mix and print that name on a window or mirror. Let this dry so you can't see it. (If the name shows too much, add a little more water to the Magic mix and try again.)

The Trick:

◼ Surprise your friends by telling them that your magical powers can make ghost writing appear. The message will probably be the name of someone at the show.
◼ Mysteriously move over to the window and breathe heavily through your mouth on the invisible name. Fog will form around the printing and the name will stand out because of your Magic mix. That's really spooky!

THE WIZARD'S POTION

Make magic water fizzle and bubble at your command.

You'll Need:

Clear glass
White vinegar
Food coloring
1 tbsp. baking soda in a bowl
Big plate or tray

The Trick:

◼ Announce that you can turn plain water into a wizard's magic potion.
◼ Present the glass, half filled with vinegar, and pretend it is water. Place this on a big plate or tray for the overflow.
◼ Dramatically add a dash of food coloring as you mumble:
"Fizzle, fizzle, fubble,
Bibble, bibble, bubble."
◼ Cast this same spell over your magic dust (baking soda) and drop the soda into the vinegar. Alakazam!
◼ Now challenge someone else to try this trick but give your volunteer real water instead.

Show Time

Master of Disguise

The octopus can change color before you can say "Abracadabra, Abracadee!" An octopus's skin is full of tiny color sacs that are controlled by muscles. The octopus can confuse its enemies by opening and closing all of these sacs so quickly that there is an instant color change. Its next trick is to disappear behind a cloud of ink. It shoots out its own black potion and makes a magic getaway behind it.

Baffling Body Tricks

All you really need is you, some friends and a little know-how.

THE HEAVY BODY TRICK
Are you heavy as a horse or light as a feather? Just move your arms a little and dare your friends to find out.

The Trick:

■ Stand upright with your arms bent and tucked into your sides, hands at your shoulders, elbows pointing to the floor.
■ Ask two strong friends to each hold one of your elbows and lift you straight up. Up you go.
■ Tell your friends that you can magically make yourself so heavy that they can't possibly lift you again.
■ This time, before they start to lift you, place your hands securely on your shoulders and stick your elbows out to the front. This time you'll stay grounded! Ta da!

Body Magic

FLOATING ARMS

Up, up, and away!

The Trick:

■ Tell a friend that you can magically raise his arms without even touching him.

■ Ask him to stand in a doorway and press the backs of his hands as hard as he can against the door frame while you count to 25.

■ Now ask him to step away from the door frame and relax. Watch out for flying arms!

PENNY PICKUP

Try to pick a penny up from this position. You will think you can but...

The Trick:

■ Challenge a friend to pick up a penny from the floor without moving his feet or bending his knees.

■ Ask him to stand with his back to the wall, feet together and heels against the wall.

■ Put a penny on the floor in front of his feet. Now watch him try!

Magic Challenge 2.

Can you pick up an empty soda bottle using only a straw? Don't touch the bottle with your hands.

See page 32 for the answer.

Tricky Fingers

Here are a few handy tricks to have up your sleeve.

TWIST AND TIE

Here's how to cross your arms and tie a knot...all in one!

The Setup:

1. Lay a scarf lengthwise in front of you, on a table.
2. Fold your arms.
3. Grasp one end of the scarf with your hand that is up and the other end with the hand that is down.
4. Firmly hold the scarf and unfold your arms. Now you have a knot in the middle.

The Trick:

■ Place the scarf in front of a friend. Ask her to fold her arms and then tie a knot. Chances are she will try but will not be able to tie the knot.
■ Now it is your turn to show your super-duper knot-tying powers.

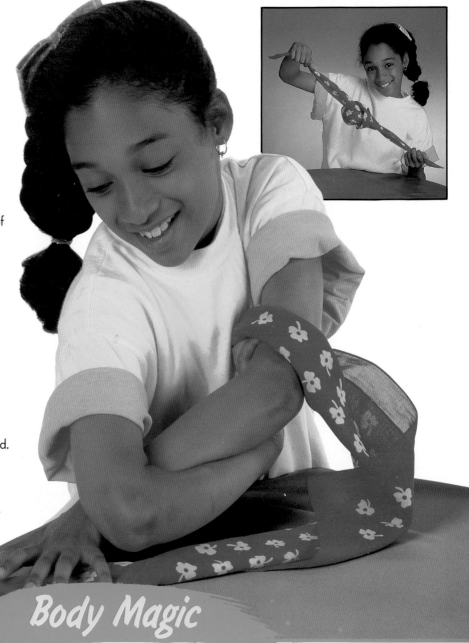

Body Magic

FINGER TWIST

SHAZAM! With one magic word you can make a friend's fingers do funny things.

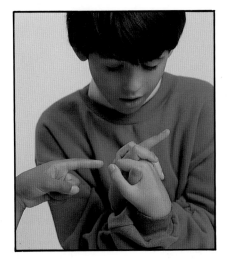

The Setup:

1. Your friend should interlock his fingers as shown.

The Trick:

■ Cast the magic spell and inform your friend that he no longer has control over his fingers.
■ Without touching him, point to one of his fingers and ask him to move it. He'll move any finger but the correct one.

Baby Fingers

Put your finger in the hand of a baby and she or he will grab on tightly. Why do their tiny fingers seem to grasp at everything? Babies can't help themselves. They are always looking for warmth and love or food. Their busy fingers keep them in touch with people who love them.

BROKEN THUMB

Thumbs up to the magician who can split a thumb in two and then magically make it one again.

The Setup:

1. Place your left hand against your waist, palm up and thumb on the outside. Now bend both your thumbs and bring them together in front of you, knuckle to knuckle. Your right thumb should look like an extension of your left thumb. (See drawing.)

2. Hide the crack where the two thumbs join with your right index finger.

3. Keep your index finger in front as a screen and move your right hand to the right to separate your thumbs.

You must practice this in front of a mirror many times before your show. Then it will seem easy.

The Trick:

■ Amaze your audience by announcing that you can break your thumb in two.
■ Face your audience, place your thumbs and index finger in position, and slowly work your magic. This quick and easy trick can be done anytime, anywhere and your friends will love it.

Eye Puzzlers

You have to keep an eye on these puzzles!
They'll trick your eyes and fool your brain.

Tabletop Trick

Can you fit a penny on top of this table without
touching the sides? Try it and find out.

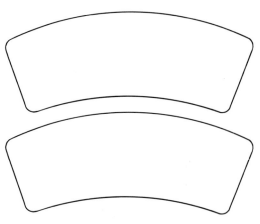

Mystifying Shapes

Which shape is larger?

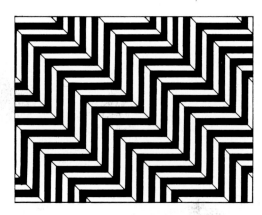

Puzzling Pattern

What happens to the pattern when you stare at it?

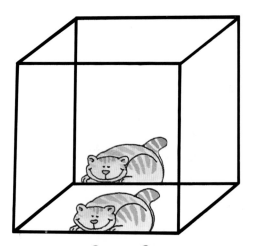

Crazy Cats

Stare at the cube for several
seconds. Which cat is closer?

Body Magic

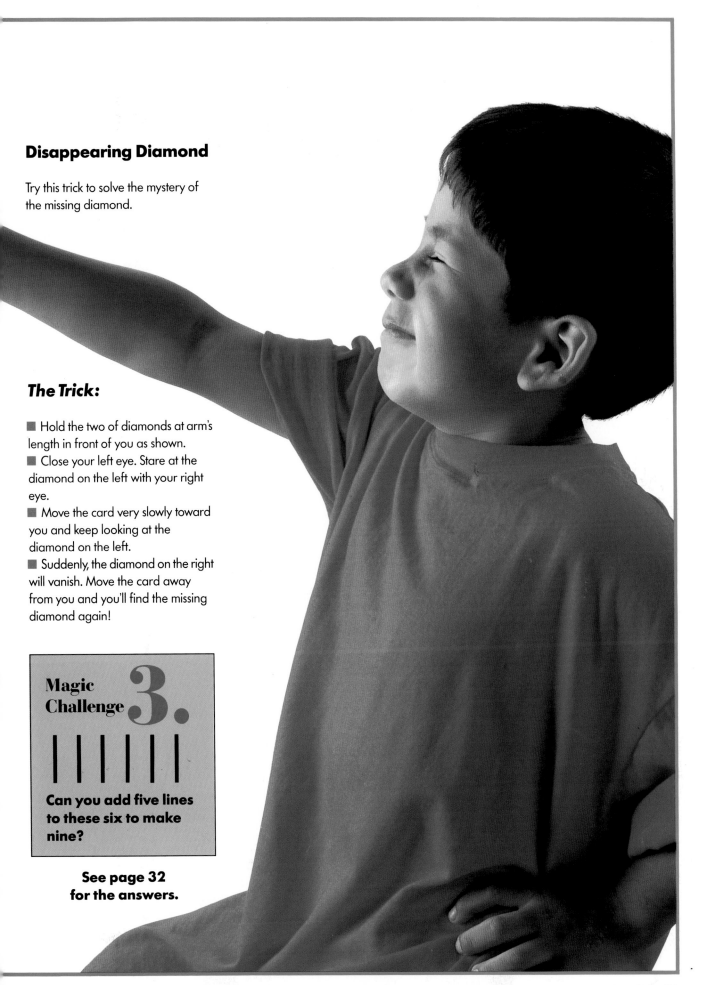

Disappearing Diamond

Try this trick to solve the mystery of the missing diamond.

The Trick:

■ Hold the two of diamonds at arm's length in front of you as shown.

■ Close your left eye. Stare at the diamond on the left with your right eye.

■ Move the card very slowly toward you and keep looking at the diamond on the left.

■ Suddenly, the diamond on the right will vanish. Move the card away from you and you'll find the missing diamond again!

Magic Challenge 3.

Can you add five lines to these six to make nine?

See page 32 for the answers.

Fantastic Fortune Cake

Bake a chocolate chip Fortune Cake and invite your friends to munch away and find their fortune.

You'll Need:

1/2 cup butter
1 cup white sugar
2 eggs
1 tsp vanilla
1 tsp baking soda
1 tsp baking powder
1 cup sour cream or yogurt
2 cups flour
2 cups chocolate chips
Mixing bowls, measuring cups and
    spoons
Greased bundt cake pan
Paper
Waxed paper
Oven preheated to 350°F (Ask an
    adult to help you.)

3 is your lucky number

Something exciting will happen today

Here's How:

■ Make your cake following these steps. Cream together the butter and sugar. Add other ingredients in the order listed and mix well with a spoon. Pour into the greased cake pan. Bake for 40 to 45 minutes. Cool, then tip out of the pan onto a dish.

Fortune Fun

Something exciting will happen today...

Wonder Powder

Baking soda is the "magic" ingredient that made your cake rise. Here are some other amazing things it can do:

Shine some silver
Scrub a sink
Refresh a refrigerator
Remove a carpet stain
And even clean your teeth!

■ Cut small up-and-down slits around the outside of the cake so each fortune will have a secret slot.
■ Write fortunes on small pieces of paper and wrap each in waxed paper.
■ Slip a fortune into every slot. Then ice the cake with your favorite icing.
■ Now celebrate the end of your show with a big surprise!

MYSTIC MUFFINS

Mystic Muffins are great for magicians on the move. Take them on a trip or tuck them in your lunch box. They'll be a treat wherever you go!

Here's How:

■ Follow your favorite muffin recipe or make the recipe on page 18.
■ Line a muffin pan with paper cupcake holders.
■ Put a wrapped-up fortune in each paper holder.
■ Pour in the muffin mix and bake.

Fast Fortune Flicker

Who needs a crystal ball? Become a fortune teller by making your very own Fortune Flicker.

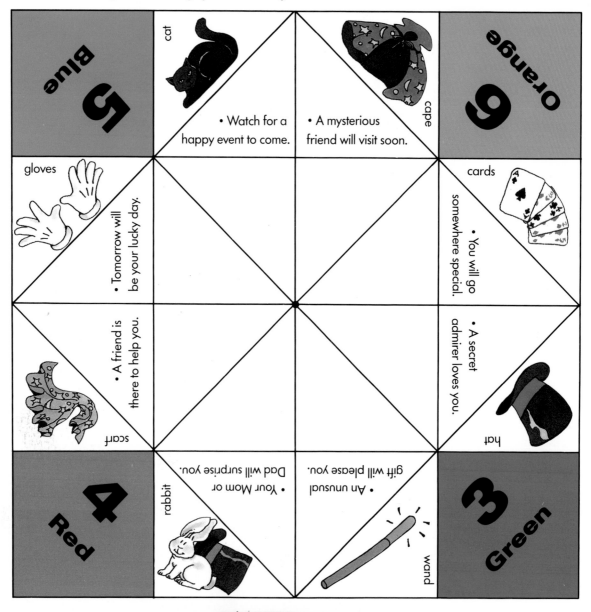

- cat
- cape
- Blue
- 5
- Orange
- 6
- • Watch for a happy event to come.
- • A mysterious friend will visit soon.
- gloves
- cards
- • Tomorrow will be your lucky day.
- • You will go somewhere special.
- • A friend is there to help you.
- • A secret admirer loves you.
- scarf
- hat
- • Your Mom or Dad will surprise you.
- • An unusual gift will please you.
- rabbit
- wand
- Red
- 4
- Green
- 3

Fortune Fun

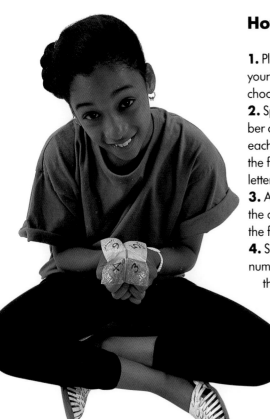

How to Play It

1. Place your fingers and thumbs in your Fortune Flicker. Ask a friend to choose one of the squares.

2. Spell the color or count the number of the chosen square and, for each count or letter, open or close the flicker. Leave it open on the last letter or number.

3. Ask your friend to choose one of the objects shown in the center of the flicker.

4. Spell the word or count the number out loud. Open and close the flicker as you did the first time.

5. Ask your friend to choose another object.

6. Unfold the flap of the object chosen and read the fortune.

How to Make It

1. Trace the pattern and lines shown here onto a square piece of paper. Write in the fortunes, color the squares, and draw the objects. (You can copy the ones here or make up your own!)

2. Turn the square over and trace the center dot onto that blank side. Fold each of the four corners in to the new center dot.

3. Turn back over and again fold all four new corners in to the center.

4. Now fold the square in half in one direction, then unfold and fold in half in the other direction.

5. Slip your index finger and thumb of each hand under the four colored flaps. Squeeze your thumbs and fingers together. Open and close the flicker by separating your fingers and thumbs first sideways and then back-to-front.

Superstitious?

You're walking along the street and a black cat crosses in front of you. Is this a sign of good or bad luck? In parts of North America, a black cat is thought to bring bad luck. In England, Japan, and parts of Europe, however, seeing a black cat means good fortune will come your way!

The 1, 2, 3 Card Trick

Presto, find-o, alamazoo!
The right card turns up every time for you.

The Trick:

■ Chant mysteriously to your friends, "Presto, find-o, alamazoo! I'm sure to find the card for you."

1. Count out 21 cards from a deck. Place them face down, in three piles of seven cards each.

2. Pick up one of the piles of cards in front of you. Fan the seven cards out face up so everyone can see them.

3. Ask someone to mentally choose a card and remember it. (He or she may tell the rest of the audience, but the magician must not know.)

4. Put the deck back together, placing the pile with the secret card in between the other two piles.

5. Deal the cards face up in three piles of seven cards each. Be sure to move from left to right, putting one card on each pile each time you deal.

6. Ask the friend to point to the pile that contains the secret card.

7. Gather the cards up again, carefully keeping the pile with the secret card between the other two.

8. Deal the cards into a single pile, but as you pick up each card pretend you are weighing it to receive the magic vibrations. Count the cards silently.

9. Then "Ta da!" Show the secret card. It will always be the eleventh one.

Magic Challenge 4.

Line up six glasses and fill the first three with water. Now try to move just one glass so that the pattern of glasses is full, empty, full, empty, full, empty.

```
 ___  ___  ___   __   __   __
|≈≈≈||≈≈≈||≈≈≈| |  | |  | |  |
 1    2    3    4    5    6
```

See page 32 for the answer.

Card Capers

Check the Deck

Practice these card tricks. Then perform them
in your magic show or save them for a rainy day.

WHERE'S JACK?

Who can find the Jack?

You'll Need:

The Jack and three other cards from
an old deck of cards
Scissors
Glue

The Setup:

1. Cut the Jack from the bottom left
corner to the middle at the top of
the card. (See picture.)
2. Glue the left piece from the Jack
at an angle across the face of
another card.
3. Carefully arrange the two remaining cards on top of each other and
treat them as one.
4. Now place these two cards partly
over the Jack so the Jack is just

peeking out. (See picture.) You are
holding three cards but only two
can be seen along with the fake
Jack.

The Trick:

■ Hold up the cards
with the Jack in the
middle. Tell a long
story about Jack
and how he
often disappears. Ask
everyone to
keep an eye
on him.

■ Close the cards. Turn them upside
down (not around) to face you. Fan
them out. Jack should be gone.
■ Invite someone to point to the
back of the card they think is Jack.
But when you turn the cards to face
them, Jack isn't there at all!

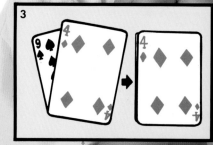

Card Capers

THE BLACK AND RED TRICK

This trick is quick and easy, but your friends will never guess the secret.

The Trick:

■ Before you start the trick, fix your deck. Pile all the red cards at one end of the deck and the black ones at the other.

■ Turn the deck face down. Fan out the red cards and keep the black ones tucked at the bottom of the deck.

■ Ask a friend to pull a card out, look at it, and remember it.

■ Meanwhile, close the deck in your hand. Fan the cards out again (still face down), but this time fan out the black cards.

■ Tell your friend to put the card back in the deck.

■ Look mysteriously through the deck and you will easily find the one red card among the black ones. Pretend that your magic powers have guided you to the secret card.

Playing Cards

Take a good look at the clothes on the Queen and King in your deck. They're wearing the court costume of King Henry VII of England. He lived over four hundred years ago. And playing cards have been around even longer than that! There are hundreds of different card games, and some people even "tell fortunes" with special tarot cards.

Mind Reading

"Mirror, mirror on the wall, Who is the best magician of all?"

Try this amazing, mind-boggling trick and the answer might be "You!"

Number Telepathy

A whiz kid and a mind reader, too? Test your numbers know-how with this trick.

The Setup:

1. Practice with a partner the secret sign you will use to pass the correct number along.
2. Gently place your hands on each side of your partner's head. Your fingers should be over his ears and your palms covering the back of his jaw.

3. Now your partner makes short chewing motions with his teeth together and his mouth closed. You can feel it but others can't see it.
4. Count the number of "chews" and you will have the answer. If he "chews" ten times, the number is ten.

Magic Challenge

Pick any number. Now double it and add five. Add twelve. Take away three. Now halve it. Take away the number you first picked. What will the answer always be?

See page 32 for the answer.

The Trick:

■ Who will believe that a Master Magician can feel numbers right through people's heads?
■ Ask your friends to decide, while you are out of the room, on a number between one and ten.
■ When you return, move mysteriously about the room, feeling people's heads and faces until you come to your partner. Pretend it takes a few minutes for you to feel the right impulses from the brain.
■ Your partner gives you the correct number with your secret sign. Once again you prove to be the one and only, the amazing Master Magician!

Mind Magic

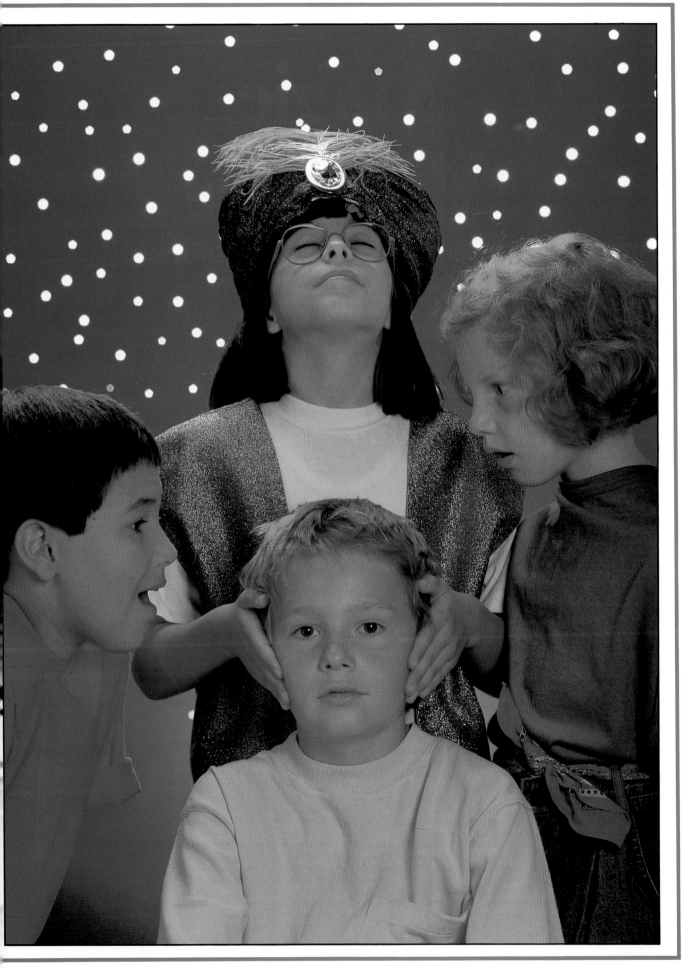

Magic Messages

Try these tricks, then think up some new ones for your magic message box.

THE KNOW-IT-ALL BOX

You'll pick the right answer from this box every time.

You'll Need:

A big cardboard box
Bright wrapping paper
Colored or shiny paper
Paints
Glue or clear tape
Scissors
An envelope
Pencil and small pieces of paper

The Setup:

1. Cover your box with bright paper. Decorate it with colored-paper cut-outs or paints.

2. Draw a picture of a dog on a piece of paper and write the word "dog" underneath it. Stuff this in an envelope and seal it.

The Trick:

■ Tell your audience that inside the sealed envelope is the name of an animal and announce that your Know-it-all Box will be able to figure out what that animal is.

■ Ask your audience to help by naming some animals for you to write on the small pieces of paper and put into the box.

■ Chances are that someone will call out "dog," but if you want to be doubly sure, plant a friend in the audience to say it.

Mind Magic

Brain Power

The brain is an amazing computer. Once something is filed in your memory it is there for good. When you forget something, you only "forget" how to find it in the large storage system of the brain. Trying to remember something small or a few years old is a bit like looking for your frisbee after not using it for the whole winter.

■ The trick is to write "dog," instead of the audience's suggestions, on every piece of paper!
■ Chant: "Hocus Pocus, Jimminy Occus," and wave your hands in the air. Swoop down and pull out a name from the box. It's "dog!"
■ Now the tension mounts. Open the sealed envelope and…Surprise! The Know-it-all Box knows all.

COLOR VISION

This famous trick is for the magician with eyes in the back of her head.

You'll Need:

The Know-it-all Box
Box of crayons

The Setup:

Place the Know-it-all Box in front of you and dump the crayons inside.

The Trick:

■ Casually announce that you can see color through the eyes in the back of your head.

■ Turn your back to the audience. Ask a volunteer to show everyone the crayons in the box and then choose one.
■ Direct her to place the crayon in your hands, which are held behind your back.
■ As you turn around to face the audience, secretly dig one finger- or thumbnail into the crayon.
■ Keep the crayon behind your back in one hand. Bring the other hand forward – the one with the crayon bits under your nails.
■ Pretend you are trying to "see" through the back of your head and move your free hand up to your forehead. Meanwhile, have a peek at the color on your nail.
■ Suddenly, you are struck with a color vision and you magically call out the color. It's true! Magicians do have eyes in the back of their heads.

Trick Tips

Whether you want to put on a full magic show or just impress your friends and family, these tips will help make your performance even more impressive.

1. Practice, practice, practice! Try your tricks in front of a mirror.

2. Never tell how a trick is done and never do a trick twice. You'll lose the magic of it all.

3. Mix your tricks so your audience is surprised with a variety of magic. You might move from a card trick to mind reading to a vanishing coin trick.

Abracadabra

"Abracadabra" is a very, very old magical charm. In the ancient Orient people thought that chanting this special word would bring help from kind spirits to ward off sickness. Through the Middle Ages, "Abracadabra" became used more generally in magic. Chant it when you do some of your more mysterious tricks.

Mind Magic

4. Find a table for your show and cover it with a cloth that reaches down to the ground.

5. Set up your tricks well in advance with your supplies arranged under the table ready to be used.

7. Keep your audience in front of your table, not to the sides.

8. Be sure to look at your audience and speak clearly. This is your show!

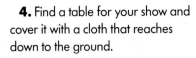

6. Use hand gestures to distract or add to the drama. Frown, pause, stare, or chitchat to set the magic tone. Remember, you are the actor.

9. Start your act with a trick that is quick and exciting. End your performance with your best trick.

10. Learn some jokes to fill in the time between tricks.

11. Use special effects to set a magical mood. Blow bubbles or dried dandelions around for friends to catch and make magic wishes on.

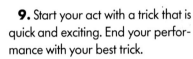

DISAPPEARING PENNY TRICK

12. Have lots of fun!

Answers

Eye Puzzlers

These images, called "optical illusions," are specially designed to create visually deceptive impressions of size, dimension, and movement.

Tabletop Trick

The penny won't fit because the picture of a table is a parallelogram, not a rectangle as a real table is.

Crazy Cats

If you look at the cube long enough, each cat seems to take a turn being closer than the other.

Mystifying Shapes

Although the bottom shape *seems* to be larger, both are exactly the same size.

Puzzling Pattern

The pattern seems to vibrate and also appears three-dimensional.

Challenges

Magic Challenge 1.

Place a coin from either end on top of the middle one.

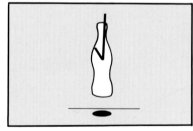

Magic Challenge 4.

Pick up glass 2 and pour the water from it into glass 5. Then return glass 2 to its place.

Magic Challenge 2.

Bend the straw about three quarters of the way down. Push the bent end into the empty soda bottle. Make sure the bent straw is pressing against the inside of the bottle. Now hold the long end of the straw and carefully lift the bottle. Ta da!

See diagram above right.

Magic Challenge 3.

Magic Challenge 5.

The answer is always seven!